ZERO WASTE

60 Recipes for a Waste-Free Kitchen

Photographs and Recipes
CINZIA TRENCHI

Project Editor
VALERIA MANFERTO DE FABIANIS

Graphic Design
PAOLA PIACCO

Contents

Fruit-Based Recipes 108

Leftover Bread or Other Food 142

Index of Ingredients 158

The Author 160

! *All of the ingredients, both fresh and dried, must be organic*
. *and preservative-free.*

The Secret Resources of Vegetables

We are used to considering food as something "easy" in our life: easy to buy, easy to eat, easy to waste. A fuel source that can be easily acquired, based on appearance, shape, and color. Often, however, we don't think about the effort, commitment, and resources invested in producing the fruit or vegetables we buy, just as we don't give proper consideration to the amount of time and miles between the products being harvested and them arriving in our kitchen. Then, when it is time to eat those products, we often unknowingly, or out of habit, waste a large part of them, without even thinking about the nutritional benefits that the "scraps" — skins, stems, seeds — could offer us. Take melon, for example: we throw away the rind and seeds, and consequently the flesh attached to them. But, with a little effort, these parts can become excellent ingredients for making a delicious jam, while the seeds — dried in the oven, lightly toasted, and then salted — are perfect for enriching bread and flatbreads. And you'll be surprised what you can do with corn scraps. The husks make exceptional wraps for flavorful fillings, made with surprising ingredients like parsley stalks and onion, eggplant, or tomato skins, while the cob can be used to make a wonderful vegetable stock for soups or risottos. As long as you choose your products carefully — freshness and quality are fundamental — the resources of vegetables are inexhaustible. You can make a superb pesto with carrot tops, provided they are fresh and green. Leathery artichoke petals can be transformed into a tasty stuffing for ravioli, while turnip and radish leaves add that extra touch to any salad or soup. Deep fried pumpkin skins are truly scrumptious, and watermelon rind compote is a mouth-watering condiment for meatballs or cheese.

Of course, the genuineness of vegetables depends on their origin and on how dedicated producers are to their farming practices, which should preferably be organic or biodynamic. If we want to use every part of our fruit and vegetables, the skins must be unadulterated and not contaminated by pesticides. It is also better if they haven't been stored in the refrigerator for a long time, are in season, and are grown locally. Always read the ingredients when using protein-based scraps — for example, shrimp and shrimp scampi shells, or the shells of crustaceans in general — because sulfites are often used to preserve color and extend shelf life. You should therefore choose foods that are as natural as possible, as well as free of additives. It is important to understand that by using every part of a fruit or vegetable, or by discarding as little as possible, they will provide us with all the nutrients they contain. We now know that, in most cases, the properties are concentrated in the skin and seeds, parts that — if properly prepared — can become excellent, zero-cost appetizers, snacks, and ingredients for desserts. Therefore, using food scraps will gradually help you save money, as well as reduce the number of garbage bags you use. Sometimes, the only thing holding us back is not knowing how to use the discarded parts of the vegetables. In the collective imagination, waste is equivalent to "not good" or "not very healthy," but, for example, if you roast and crumble the white piths of bell peppers, together with the seeds, you can make an exquisite pasta sauce or use them as seasoning for stewed vegetables, and potato skins are truly sublime when fried. Perhaps, by trying our hand at a different way of using food — one that our grandmothers were well acquainted with — we can break the daily habits that make us do everything on automatic pilot.

And this will open the door to a whole new, unexplored world that may pleasantly surprise you — because, in addition to tasting good, dishes made with food scraps also look great. This book is divided into topics and illustrated with original photographs. It begins with fact sheets on the fruit and vegetables used in the recipes, offering suggestions on how to use and dry the scraps, and describing their properties. The following sections contain recipes for simple, quick dishes, which are both full of goodness and pleasing to the eye. The aim of this book is to provide appetizing and easy-to-make recipes that use the parts of fruit and vegetables we usually discard — broccoli stems, the outer leaves of celery, the peel of grapefruit and orange, and the rind of watermelon, to name but a few. It will also show you how citrus peel, for example, can be used to flavor cookies, salt, and condiments. There are four sections with recipes for snacks, appetizers, first courses, main courses, side dishes, condiments, cookies, buns, cakes, breads, and even a liqueur, all illustrated with beautiful photographs. The first section focuses on vegetables, with twenty-two ideas for making the most of the parts you usually throw away. This is followed by fourteen protein-based recipes that use cheese and fish scraps. The main ingredients in the seventeen fruit-based recipes are peach and apple skins, watermelon and melon rind, and grapefruit peel, so you can create colorful, tasty, fragrant, and original dishes that will entice even the most skeptical of dinner guests! Last, but by no means least, there are seven recipes using leftover bread, rice, and pasta. All these recipes will give you an ace up your sleeve for making new and creative dishes to intrigue friends, family, or customers, and hopefully for making an ethical decision that shows respect and appreciation for both nature and yourself.

Fennel is an annual or biennial vegetable, mainly found in stores in fall and winter. It has extremely fragrant, green fronds at the top of its leaves, which are pure white. The part we usually eat is the bulb, which grows directly from the roots. Fennel is fresh and thirst-quenching, and can be eaten both raw and cooked. The tender bulb is wrapped in hard, fibrous leaves, which, when thinly sliced and dried, are excellent for enriching soups and salads. They are also ideal as a delicious accompaniment to an aperitif or to freshen your breath. Fennel has very few calories and is an ally in weight loss and detox diets, but it contains a fair amount of mineral salts such as calcium, phosphorus, sulfur, sodium, and potassium. Wash and dry the leaves thoroughly, finely chop them, and then place them in the sun. Once dried, they should be stored in a glass jar.

FENNEL

The contrast between a cucumber's silky peel and watery, crunchy flesh suggests using these parts separately. The peel should be removed with a potato peeler and then dried on parchment paper. When heated, cucumber peel curls into unusual shapes, and — in addition to tasting good — it can be used to add a touch of originality to dishes. You can make a delicious appetizer by seasoning them with salt and putting them in the oven at 350°F (180°C), while ground dried peel can be added to salads or mixed with herbs. Cucumber is rich in fiber and mucilage, which improve digestion, and it is also a diuretic. It contains several minerals, such as potassium, magnesium, calcium, sodium, phosphorus, silicon (promotes healthy hair and nails), iron, and zinc. This vegetable is low in calories, making it the perfect ally in obtaining an enviable figure!

CUCUMBER

Traditionally, we eat the immature flower head of an artichoke, known as the heart, the petals of which are more tender and sweeter than the fibrous, leathery outer ones. Some gourmets also use the stems, but there are few recipes that use the whole vegetable. However, it is worth knowing that both the leaves and the tough, fibrous petals can be used to make fantastic dishes, as long as you use them carefully. Artichoke tends to oxidize very quickly, becoming bitter and unpleasant. Once trimmed, it should be immediately dipped in water and lemon juice to preserve its color and give it a nice taste. The discarded petals are perfect for making soups, purées, and condiments. They are also a good source of fiber and low in calories. The leaves are excellent for making decoctions and detox drinks, as they stimulate urination and bile production in the liver. The artichoke ripens in winter, and its leaves can be dried and stored in glass jars.

ARTICHOKE

Broccoli belongs to the Cruciferae family. It is a winter vegetable, although it is in stores all year round. It is, however, better to include it in your diet during the colder months of the year. We usually eat the flower head, when the buds are still closed, and discard the tough, fibrous parts of the stem. However, when thoroughly washed and cut very thin, the stem is a great ingredient for simple, yet flavorful dishes. Basically, the seemingly tough stems become tender and soft when cooked. Even the leaves, both small and large, can complement tasty vegetable stews or soups. You can also blend the scraps after steaming them to make creamy sauces for pastas and risottos, while small leaves can also be added to mixed-leaf salads. It is best to use food scraps immediately, without drying them.

BROCCOLI

TURNIP

Brassica campestris, commonly known as turnip, is rich in potassium and low in calories. Its slightly spicy skin contains potassium, phosphorus, vitamin C, folic acid, calcium, and sodium. Furthermore, the leaves you can find sold in bunches, such as turnip tops, can be used both cooked and — if very small and tender — raw in salads. If you keep a turnip for a while, it will sprout, and the tasty leaves can be used in salads.

CELERY

Often, only the center of a celery plant is eaten, but when finely sliced and dried, even the hardest outer leaves are a surprising resource. They can be used to make mirepoix, for example, if you don't have any fresh celery on hand. Celery, including the leaves and strings, can be used in soups, stews, and salads, as it maintains its strong aromatic flavor. You can store it whole or finely chopped, to use on its own or with other vegetables when you need it.

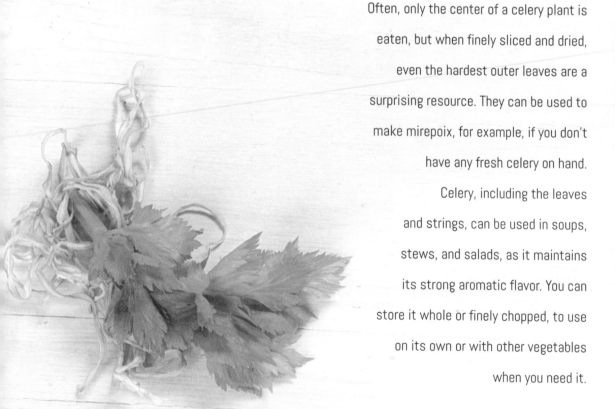

PARSLEY

The leftover stems of this aromatic herb can be dried and used with other ingredients to season mirepoix, soups, and stews. Parsley has diuretic and digestive properties, and is a valuable ingredient for our well-being. Its components include a lot of potassium, phosphorus, calcium, vitamin C, folic acid, and retinol. It can be stored in sprigs or ground, preferably in a glass jar.

PUMPKIN

Pumpkin is covered with a tough, leathery skin. If you dry it in the oven for a few hours at low temperature, together with the seeds, and then chop it up, it is a delicious ingredient for making breading, for flavoring soups or meatballs, and for a variety of other dishes.

The fresh skin is also really tasty when baked or fried.

It should be noted that to make the most of the skins, they must be thoroughly washed before being used: once dried, skins can be eaten or stored.

Potatoes come in many different colors: yellow, white, purple, pink, blue. Potatoes are the basis of many recipes, and because they are rich in starch, they are a valid substitute for pasta and bread (but with fewer calories). They are used cooked and generally peeled. This is also because, if a potato is not stored correctly, its skin can become rough, and potentially toxic buds, or "eyes," can emerge: most of the solanine, a toxic substance present in potatoes, is concentrated in the skin. If you want to use all the parts of a potato, it must be fresh and turgid, without any wrinkles, bumps, or shoots (shoots must never be used). Once it has been thoroughly washed and dried, the skin can be used to make soups or deep fried, which can make a tasty and original dish, especially if the potatoes are different colors. Potato skin is rich in fiber and contains potassium, manganese, phosphorus, calcium, and folic acid.

POTATO

The tomato belongs to the Solanaceae family, and it needs heat to ripen: it is strictly a summer fruit and is best used during this season. It should not be eaten when green because it may still contain (toxic) solanine. The skin is often removed because it doesn't amalgamate with sauces and dips; however, it is rich in lycopene and should therefore be kept and dried. Place the skins in the sun on a wooden board or parchment paper; they will become a dry and crumbly film in just a few hours. This film is perfect for grinding and using to enrich pasta dishes, risottos, and salads: a small pinch is enough to transform a dish into a highly original delicacy! Tomato skins can also be mixed with garlic, onion, and aromatic herbs to make a condiment, perfect for topping a slice of bread when you want a snack.

TOMATO

Garlic starts to germinate a few months after it has been harvested: scientific research has shown that the shoots contain all the properties of a mature bulb and that they increase antioxidant activity. If you plant a clove in a pot, it won't be long before you have a plant with the same characteristics as the bulb: the same freshness and the same antibiotic properties. The shoot has an intense flavor and can be used both fresh and dry. If left to grow, it will produce a small seedling, whose roots and scapes can also be used. When freshly cut, the scapes are really tasty, and they add a delicate flavor to soups, fish, or meat. The garlic shoot can be dried, finely chopped, and combined with other ingredients such as parsley, tomato skins, and bell peppers.

GARLIC

Whether ripe or sprouting, onion lends itself to an infinite range of culinary possibilities. The dry outer leaves, which are generally discarded, can add the final touch to a condiment made with other herbs. They can also be ground and used in soups and broth-based soups — miso soup, for example — sauces, minestrones, and omelets. Sprouting onions can be planted and left to grow: you can then cut and use the sprouts instead of a bulb. If you dry and crumble the green leaves and outer skins, you will have an excellent onion substitute for making mirepoix, condiments, and oils. Once dried, the scraps can be kept whole and then crumbled and mixed with other ingredients when needed. Thanks to its purifying and detoxifying properties, onion is considered a natural drug, and it is believed to help restore healthy gut flora.

ONION

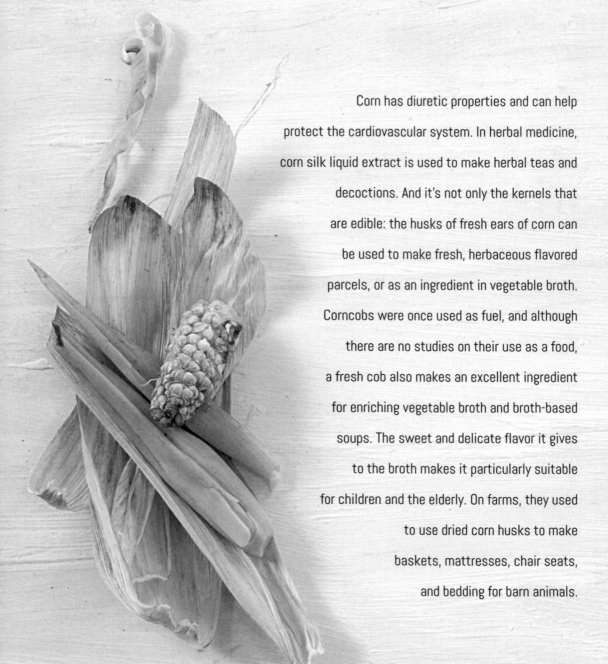

Corn has diuretic properties and can help protect the cardiovascular system. In herbal medicine, corn silk liquid extract is used to make herbal teas and decoctions. And it's not only the kernels that are edible: the husks of fresh ears of corn can be used to make fresh, herbaceous flavored parcels, or as an ingredient in vegetable broth. Corncobs were once used as fuel, and although there are no studies on their use as a food, a fresh cob also makes an excellent ingredient for enriching vegetable broth and broth-based soups. The sweet and delicate flavor it gives to the broth makes it particularly suitable for children and the elderly. On farms, they used to use dried corn husks to make baskets, mattresses, chair seats, and bedding for barn animals.

CORN

Allium porrum belongs to the same family as garlic and onion, and its flavor is reminiscent of the latter, although far more delicate. In cooking, the softer white part is usually used, but the more fibrous green part is just as good for using in soups and minestrones. Both the inner stalk and outer leaves of this vegetable are low in calories and rich in fiber, minerals, and vitamins. Leek can be found ripe both in summer and winter. You can cook the green scraps and very fibrous outer leaves with the soft, delicate white part, and then dry them. Once dried, you can cut them into small pieces and then crumble or grind them. They can be stored in a glass jar or a food bag. They are ideal for enriching condiments and using as an aromatic base for mirepoix, as well as for flavoring soups and stewed vegetables.

LEEK

Carrot is an exceptional vegetable, and its green tops can be eaten as well as the root. The leaves are generally removed before the carrots are sold because they deteriorate much faster than the root. It is always better to buy carrots that still have their tops because they are a sign of freshness. Leaves can be cut off the root and eaten fresh, added to salads, chopped into omelets, or finely chopped to make an original pesto. Any excess leaves can easily be dried in the sun or in a food dehydrator, and then stored in a glass jar. They can be chopped and sprinkled onto soups and broths to give them a touch of spiciness, or ground and mixed with herbs to create original condiments that are aromatic and full of flavor. Fresh leaves are rich in chlorophyll, which is believed to energize the body, stimulate the immune system, and help purify the liver.

CARROT

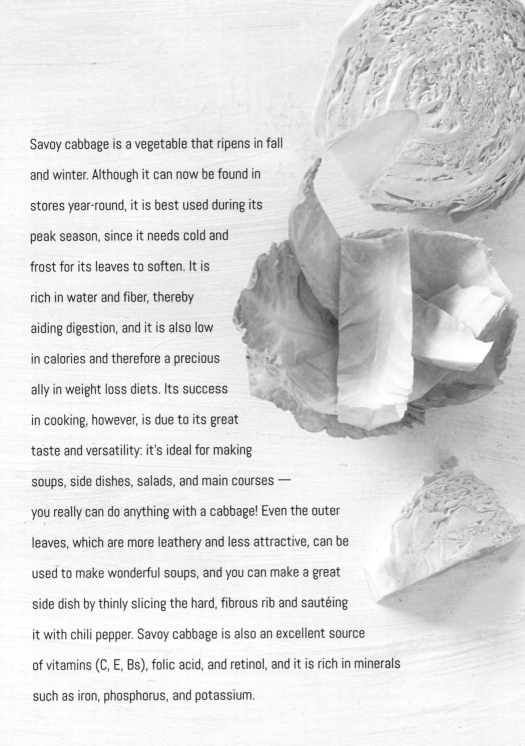

Savoy cabbage is a vegetable that ripens in fall and winter. Although it can now be found in stores year-round, it is best used during its peak season, since it needs cold and frost for its leaves to soften. It is rich in water and fiber, thereby aiding digestion, and it is also low in calories and therefore a precious ally in weight loss diets. Its success in cooking, however, is due to its great taste and versatility: it's ideal for making soups, side dishes, salads, and main courses — you really can do anything with a cabbage! Even the outer leaves, which are more leathery and less attractive, can be used to make wonderful soups, and you can make a great side dish by thinly slicing the hard, fibrous rib and sautéing it with chili pepper. Savoy cabbage is also an excellent source of vitamins (C, E, Bs), folic acid, and retinol, and it is rich in minerals such as iron, phosphorus, and potassium.

SAVOY CABBAGE

JERUSALEM ARTICHOKE

Jerusalem artichoke skin is very like that of a potato: when cooked, it becomes darker and much harder than the soft, light-colored flesh. Once removed from the tuber, it can be fried or used to make mouth-watering, creamy sauces. Jerusalem artichoke is lumpy and uneven, and it must be cleaned thoroughly to remove all the residues of soil on the skin.

BELL PEPPER

After trimming a bell pepper, you can keep the seeds, placenta, and any excess parts that you don't need for your recipe. These leftover parts can then be cut into thin strips and small pieces, placed on a plate, and then left to dry in the sun for a day. You can make a spicy condiment by mixing them whole, or ground, with some chili peppers: just a pinch is enough to give dishes a touch of color and extra taste.

RADISH

Radish belongs to the Cruciferae family and
is low in calories. In addition to its amazing
tasting root, it has delicious leaves that you can
use to make tasty salads. Leaves are extremely
delicate and have a very high water content.
They must first be washed by soaking them
in cold water, then drained in a colander and
spread out on a kitchen towel to dry. If you want
to keep them for a few days, you have to wrap
them in a cloth and put them in a plastic bag.

EGGPLANT

A large part of the fiber and anthocyanins in eggplant
is concentrated in the skin. The skin, therefore, contains
important nutritional properties, and so it is best not to
discard it. Once removed from the flesh,
just cut the skin into small strips and
place them in the sun to dry.
The result is an original and
tasty ingredient. Eggplant
skin is considered important
for our well-being, as it is high
in potassium, phosphorus, and
folic acid. The dried skin can be
kept in a glass jar.

Lemon is a fruit with a kaleidoscopic nature: it can be used as a dressing, as a remedy for small ailments, and as an ingredient in cakes and desserts. It has always been appreciated for its juice, but the peel is by no means less valued. Grated lemon peel gives an amazing aroma and delicious flavor to pastry cream, for example, and you can make an original condiment by adding it to salt. Although we are immediately captivated by its taste, it is worth knowing that the essential oil contained in the peel has many properties: it is antiseptic and balsamic; it can be used as a natural antibiotic, bactericide, and fungicide; and the flavonoids it contains appear to stimulate blood vessels. Furthermore, most of the vitamin C present in the fruit is concentrated in the peel. With fresh lemon peel, you can make scrumptious jellies or limoncello liqueur, while finely cut dried peel can be used to flavor breading, meatballs, croquettes, and, of course, salt.

LEMON

Fig skin can often cause irritation if it is not ripe enough, and when the fruit is fresh, the fibrous consistency of its skin is often unwelcome when combined with the succulent flesh. Conversely, the skin of dried figs is nice and sweet, and has a wonderful texture. Dried figs are ideal for using in cookies, cakes, jellies, smoothies, and bread, and an excellent ingredient for creating original dishes as well as a delicious snack. Being seasonal in the summer, drying the skins is very simple: just put them out in the blazing hot sun to dry. Dried fig skin is soft and slightly supple. Dried figs are best stored in paper bags, but the skins should be used within a couple of months. The whole fruit helps improve digestion, and thanks to its fiber, it can help lower cholesterol. It contains potassium, calcium, phosphorus, B vitamins, and vitamins C, A, and E.

FIG

Orange peel has a slightly bitter taste, lessened a little by its tantalizing fresh aroma; it has always been used to flavor drinks. It is a winter fruit that provides many health benefits. It is high in flavonoids, which help reduce body fat, and it is said that a hot drink made with orange peel can help weight loss because it speeds up the metabolism. It is therefore important to use all of the fruit: after juicing the orange, remove the white pith from the peel, which can then be used in a variety of recipes. It can be used fresh, for example, grated in cookies, pastry creams, and cakes, or dried to make fantastic drinks and flours. To dry the peel, you can leave it in the oven for about two hours at 120°F (50°C), dry it on a heater (in this case the smell of oranges will fill the room), or use a food dehydrator. It should be kept in a glass jar.

ORANGE

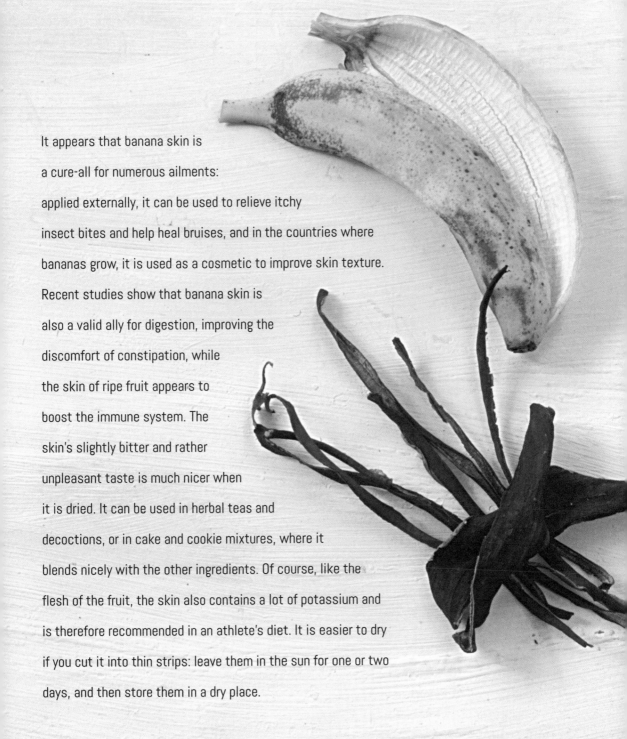

It appears that banana skin is
a cure-all for numerous ailments:
applied externally, it can be used to relieve itchy
insect bites and help heal bruises, and in the countries where
bananas grow, it is used as a cosmetic to improve skin texture.
Recent studies show that banana skin is
also a valid ally for digestion, improving the
discomfort of constipation, while
the skin of ripe fruit appears to
boost the immune system. The
skin's slightly bitter and rather
unpleasant taste is much nicer when
it is dried. It can be used in herbal teas and
decoctions, or in cake and cookie mixtures, where it
blends nicely with the other ingredients. Of course, like the
flesh of the fruit, the skin also contains a lot of potassium and
is therefore recommended in an athlete's diet. It is easier to dry
if you cut it into thin strips: leave them in the sun for one or two
days, and then store them in a dry place.

BANANA

Tangerine is one of the sweetest and most high-calorie citrus fruits, and it is deliciously fragrant and thirst-quenching. The peel is generally discarded, which is a shame because it has many health benefits: when used in an infusion or decoction, for example, it can help reduce inflammation and aid digestion. It can also be used to flavor desserts, cakes, and pastry creams, and to make liqueurs and elixirs. To dry the peel, place it on a baking tray and leave it in the oven for about two hours at 120°F (50°C). Once dehydrated, it can be ground or coarsely chopped, and then used to enrich fish-based dishes and salads, or to flavor drinks and condiments. Chopped dried peel should be stored in a glass jar, whereas whole peel should be kept in paper food bags.

TANGERINE

Mango is an exotic fruit, and it has therefore traveled many miles to arrive in our stores: it is therefore best to choose mangoes that were grown as close as possible to where we live. Make sure that the fruit is organic and that it has not been treated with preservatives. After washing it thoroughly, separate the flesh from the skin, and then dry the latter. It is best to dry the skins in the sun because even on the hottest summer days, the sun's temperature is constant and more natural than the heat provided by household appliances, although they are still a good alternative. In addition to being decorative, the dry skin still has a wonderful scent. Whether finely or coarsely chopped, it is a fantastic ingredient for flavoring cookies, cakes, salt, fish, and salads. Although the fruit is in stores all year round, it is preferable to buy it when it's in season.

MANGO

Grapefruit peel is rich in essential oils that are believed to help with depression. Its slightly bitter taste lends itself well to recipes for candied peel and jellies. After drinking the healthy fresh-squeezed grapefruit juice, which thanks to the bromelain it contains is beneficial for weight loss and stimulating the digestive system, the particularly bitter albedo must be separated from the peel. The fresh peel is ideal for using in cakes and desserts. To dry the peel, leave it in the oven for about two hours at 120°F (50°C), turning the pieces over regularly, or — if it is hot enough — sun-dry them. You can also use household appliances (in this case, follow the instructions for the times provided by the manufacturer). With chopped or ground dry peel, you can flavor oils, condiments in general, salt, and desserts.

GRAPEFRUIT

This summer fruit is characterized by a fuzzy skin that often causes irritation. These fuzzy hairs can be removed by washing the fruit vigorously, but for those who really are reluctant to eat the whole peach, it is worth knowing that most of the vitamins, fiber, and mineral salts are concentrated in the skin. That unpleasant sensation that is felt when eating the skin can be overcome by drying it. Place it on a sheet of parchment paper, and leave it in the hot sun for a day or two. Dry peach skin is a surprisingly good ingredient for snacks, fruit salads, cakes, and cookies. Its slightly supple consistency makes it a healthy substitute for candy and gum, and ideal as a healthy snack for children, and recent studies have also shown that a peach's powerful antioxidant properties, which help the cardiovascular system function correctly, are concentrated in the skin.

PEACH

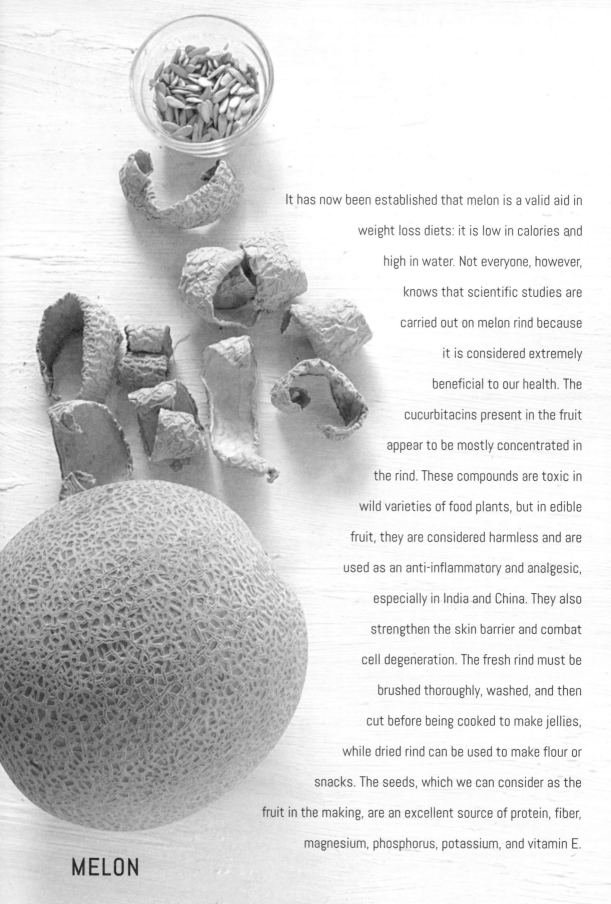

It has now been established that melon is a valid aid in weight loss diets: it is low in calories and high in water. Not everyone, however, knows that scientific studies are carried out on melon rind because it is considered extremely beneficial to our health. The cucurbitacins present in the fruit appear to be mostly concentrated in the rind. These compounds are toxic in wild varieties of food plants, but in edible fruit, they are considered harmless and are used as an anti-inflammatory and analgesic, especially in India and China. They also strengthen the skin barrier and combat cell degeneration. The fresh rind must be brushed thoroughly, washed, and then cut before being cooked to make jellies, while dried rind can be used to make flour or snacks. The seeds, which we can consider as the fruit in the making, are an excellent source of protein, fiber, magnesium, phosphorus, potassium, and vitamin E.

MELON

Apple peel is incredibly good, even if just
dried in the summer sun! Thanks to
its consistency, it can be chewed
for a long time, and it is great as a
snack to help stimulate saliva flow and
consequently the flow of lymph. Apple contains
many important elements, such as potassium,
phosphorus, calcium, vitamin C, and also —
depending on the color
— retinol. Research
has shown that the
maximum concentration of
nutrients is in the peel: you
should therefore choose organic
apples, and if you want to preserve
them, they must be stored in a cool, dark, and dry place.
While fresh peel can be unpleasant to chew, when it is dried,
it loses its fibrous texture and becomes pleasantly chewy,
giving you a delicate sensation of sweet freshness in your mouth.
It is also an excellent ingredient for flavoring sponge cake,
cakes, and cookies, or for adding a sweet touch
to roast pork.

APPLE

Vegetable-Based Dishes

Vegetables constitute one of the most important pillars of a healthy diet. Low in calories and rich in minerals, vitamins, and fiber, they should be a part of all meals. Each season offers us different flavors, textures, and colors, and it is impossible to imagine a dish without vegetables as a wonderful accompaniment. When cooking, we are used to sometimes wasting food, but the current trend is to re-evaluate the parts that we once threw away: leaves, roots, cores, skins. Not only should every part of a vegetable be used for its undisputed nutritional properties, but also for ethical reasons. The truth of the matter is that we often only discard the outer leaves of cabbage, fennel, celery, or artichoke — to name but a few — out of habit. From an early age, we watched our parents remove the skin and seeds of a pumpkin or throw away melon skins: more often than not, the only thing these parts were used for was to make compost. This section contains easy recipes for resurrecting what we have long, and mistakenly, considered "scraps." Both their taste and texture will reveal unexpected qualities, and — last but not least — scientific research tells us that most of the time the nutrients are concentrated in the outer part of the vegetable, the part that we often throw away. So, let's welcome cucumber, eggplant, and tomato skins into our kitchens, and use them to enrich appetizers, soups, and broths. Let's embrace new and original combinations of color and flavor, and incredibly imaginative and appetizing food made with particular respect for the environment!

DRIED BELL PEPPER SCRAPS

Easy

10 minutes

2 days

• the scraps of 2 bell peppers

Wash the bell peppers and remove their stalks.

Take all the parts that are usually discarded: placenta, seeds, and the flesh near the stalk. Cut them into small pieces, and place them on a piece of parchment paper.

Put them to dry in the sun for a couple of days, turning them over regularly. Once dried, finely chop them, and then put them in a glass jar.

You can use these scraps together with bell pepper or tomato peels to flavor oil, or to add a special finishing touch to omelets, condiments, and sauces for pasta, risotto, and vegetables.

DRIED FENNEL

Easy

10 minutes

1 day

• 8 outer fennel leaves

Wash the fennel leaves, keeping any fronds.

Dry them thoroughly, and use a mandoline or meat slicer to cut them into thin ribbons that will be easier to dry.

Place the ribbons on a piece of parchment paper, and leave them to dry in the sun for one day, turning them over regularly so that they dry evenly.

Once dried, put the pieces of fennel in a glass jar with a lid, and use them to flavor soups and salads. You can also chew them instead of candy to freshen your breath.

DRIED CELERY

Easy

10 minutes

1 day

• 10 outer celery leaves

Even when well cooked, the outer leaves of celery are very tough and unpleasant to eat. However, when thinly sliced and dried, they have a delicious aroma and are free of hard-to-chew fibers.

Trim, wash, and dry the leaves, then slice them finely with a mandoline or meat slicer. Place the celery ribbons on a piece of parchment paper, and leave them to dry in the sun for one day, turning them over regularly.

Once dried, put them in a jar. Naturally, drying times vary depending on the thickness of the ribbons: thinner pieces require less time, whereas thicker ribbons contain more liquid and therefore take longer to dry. You can use dried celery for soups, mirepoix, sauces, and roasts.

DRIED EGGPLANT SKINS

Easy

5 minutes

5–6 hours

1 hour

Whenever a recipe requires you to remove the skin of an eggplant, use a potato peeler to create ribbons, and then put them to one side. In this way, they will dry quickly, and you can use them for decorating dishes and to flavor or add a special touch to sauces and condiments.

During the summer, it takes only a few hours for the skins to dry in the sun, while for the rest of the year, you can leave them in the oven at low temperature for about an hour.

You can use the skins to flavor sauces, condiments, salads, and soups, or to make a delicious crunchy snack by adding a pinch of salt and pepper, and cooking them in the oven.

DRIED CUCUMBER PEELS

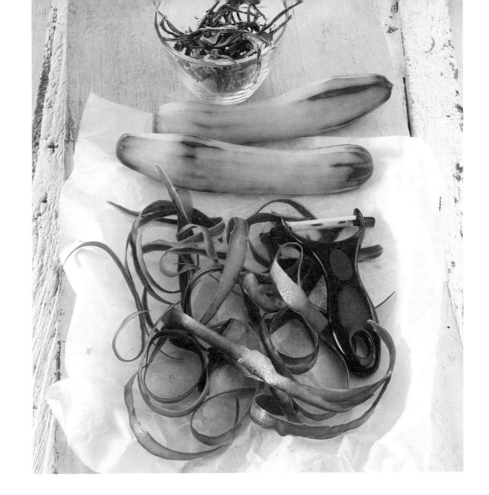

Easy

5 minutes

1 day

2 hours

The peel is often removed from cucumber because it is difficult to digest, but when it is dried, it causes less problems. As cucumber is very watery, it has to be left to dry in the sun for at least one day for the liquid to evaporate, and for you to be able to preserve it (if the season doesn't permit this, you can leave it in the oven for about two hours). The dried skin is really good when crumbled in yogurt or salads, for example, and it adds a summery touch to winter dishes.

For a tasty snack, add salt, or a pinch of spices, and cook the skins in the oven.

RADISH AND FENNEL APERITIF

2

Easy

10 minutes

• the skins of 4 fresh organic radishes
• 2 tbsp dried fennel leaves
• salt and pepper

For decorating:
• pieces of dried fennel
• dried cucumber peel
• 2 radishes

Put the radish skins, fennel leaves, 5 ice cubes, and 1/2 cup (1 dl) of water in a blender, then season with salt and pepper.

Blend until the mixture is perfectly smooth.

Pour into glasses, and decorate each glass with pieces of fennel, cucumber peel sticks, and 1 radish.

Serve immediately to enjoy the drink's refreshing effect to the fullest.

PUMPKIN AND TURNIP SKINS

4

Easy

5 minutes

10–15 minutes

- 3 1/2 oz (100 g) turnip skin
- 7 oz (200 g) pumpkin skin
- 1/2 cup (1 dl) peanut oil
- 1 tbsp dried green leek leaves
- 1 tbsp finely chopped roasted pumpkin and melon seeds
- salt and pepper

Wash, dry, and cut the peels to the desired size. Heat the oil and add the skins when it is hot, cooking the pumpkin skins first.

When they have reached the desired consistency, remove them with a slotted spoon, and drain them on paper towels.

Transfer them to a serving plate, and sprinkle with the coarsely chopped leek and finely chopped roasted seeds.

Season with salt and pepper to taste, and serve piping hot.

PUMPKIN SKIN AND SEED FLOUR

Easy

20 minutes

1 day

2 hours

• 1 pumpkin
• salt and pepper

Wash the pumpkin thoroughly, slice it, and remove the skin from the flesh. Then remove the seeds and surrounding fibers.

Arrange all the parts on a piece of greaseproof paper, and leave them in the sun. In summer, pumpkin flesh and seeds need a full day in the sun to dry completely.

Alternatively, dry them in the oven at 100–120°F (40–50°C) for 2 hours, with the door slightly open, checking on their progress from time to time.

Once the skin and seeds are dry, finely chop them, and season with salt and pepper. You can use this flour to make crackers and breadsticks, or as a condiment for pasta, soups, and rice.

SALTED CUCUMBER, EGGPLANT, CARROT, AND FENNEL SKINS

4

Easy

20 minutes

- 4 carrots, 2 purple and 2 orange
- 2 cucumbers
- 2 eggplants
- the outer leaves of 2 fennel bulbs
- salt flavored with seeds or spices

1 day

5 minutes

Wash the carrots and remove the skins with a potato peeler. Arrange the skins on a piece of parchment paper, and leave them to dry in the sun; they generally take half a day to dry completely. Once dried, store them in a glass jar.

Wash, dry, and peel the cucumbers with a potato peeler. Place the peels on a piece of parchment paper, and leave in the sun for a whole day, turning them over regularly.

Peel the eggplants and cut the skins into thin strips. Put them into a food dehydrator and follow the indicated times, or leave them to dry in the sun, turning them every now and then so that they dry completely.

Wash, dry, and thinly slice the fennel leaves using a mandoline, a meat slicer, or a very sharp knife. Place on a piece of parchment paper, and leave to dry in the sun for a whole day, turning them over regularly.

Before serving, put the skins on a baking tray, season with salt flavored with seeds or spices, and bake in the oven for 5 minutes at 400°F (200°C).

The crispy, fragrant, and appetizing skins are now ready to serve.

ROAST PUMPKIN SKINS
WITH TOMATO AND ONION

4

Easy

- approx. 10 oz (300 g) pumpkin skins
- 2 tbsp tomato skins
- 5 dried onion leaves
- 2 tbsp extra virgin olive oil
- salt and pepper

10 minutes

20 minutes

Wash the pumpkin skins thoroughly and brush with oil.
Arrange them on a baking tray lined with parchment paper.

Preheat the oven to 400°F (200°C).

Finely grind the tomato skins and onion leaves, using a mortar
and pestle or a food processor, and sprinkle the ground mixture
over the pumpkin skins. Season with salt and pepper to taste.

Cook the skins in the oven for about 20 minutes, checking them
every now and then to make sure that they're not burning.
Turn the oven off and take the skins out.

Arrange the skins on a serving plate, and serve as a snack
or with an aperitif.

PUMPKIN, LEEK, AND EGGPLANT SKIN TEMPURA

2

Easy

20 minutes

10–15 minutes

- the skin of 1 fresh eggplant
- the skin of 1 large slice of fresh pumpkin
- 4 fresh leek leaves
- 3/4 cup (100 g) whole-wheat flour
- 1/2 cup (1 dl) cold mineral water
- 1/2 cup (1 dl) peanut oil
- salt

Wash the eggplant and pumpkin skins, and trim the leek leaves. Cut into small pieces measuring 1 in (2.5 cm).

Make the batter by mixing the flour with cold water, and then add the vegetables. Heat the oil until hot, and then fry the skins a few at a time, until the batter becomes crispy, golden, and brown.

Remove the vegetables from the pan, and place them on a paper towel to absorb the excess oil.

Season with salt, and arrange the tempura on a serving plate. Serve piping hot.

DEEP-FRIED POTATO SKINS

2

Easy

5 minutes

5–7 minutes

- 4 potatoes (color of your choice)
- 1/4 cup (0.5 dl) peanut oil
- a sprig of rosemary
- salt and pepper

Only use the peels of fresh or well-preserved potatoes, free from shoots and green spots, and with a smooth surface. Wash the potatoes thoroughly, peel them, and then cut the skins so they are 2 in (5 cm) long and 1 in (2.5 cm) wide.

Heat the oil to a temperature of about 350°F (170°C), add the skins, and then fry them for about 5 minutes, stirring them regularly.

Place on a paper towel to absorb the excess oil, season with salt and pepper, sprinkle with a little rosemary, and serve immediately.

They are ideal for serving with an aperitif, and they also make a tasty snack.

CREAMY BROWN RICE SOUP WITH POTATO, CELERY, AND EGGPLANT SKINS

4

Easy

15 minutes

1 hour

- 1/2 cup (100 g) brown rice
- the skins of 4 medium to large potatoes
- 3–4 celery stalks with leaves
- 4 spring onion stalks
- 4 tbsp extra virgin olive oil
- 4 slices of stale bread
- 4 handfuls of dried eggplant skins
- salt and pepper

Wash the potato skins, celery, and spring onion stalks. Cut them into pieces, and then boil them in 6 1/4 cups (1 1/2 l) of water with the rice, for about 1 hour over low heat.

Season with salt and pepper to taste during cooking. Remove from the heat when the liquid has reduced to about 2/3, and cover. Blend the mixture until it is soft, smooth, and creamy.

Toast the bread in the oven for a few minutes at 400°F (200°C).

Serve the soup piping hot, drizzled with oil, and decorated with the toasted bread and dried eggplant skins.

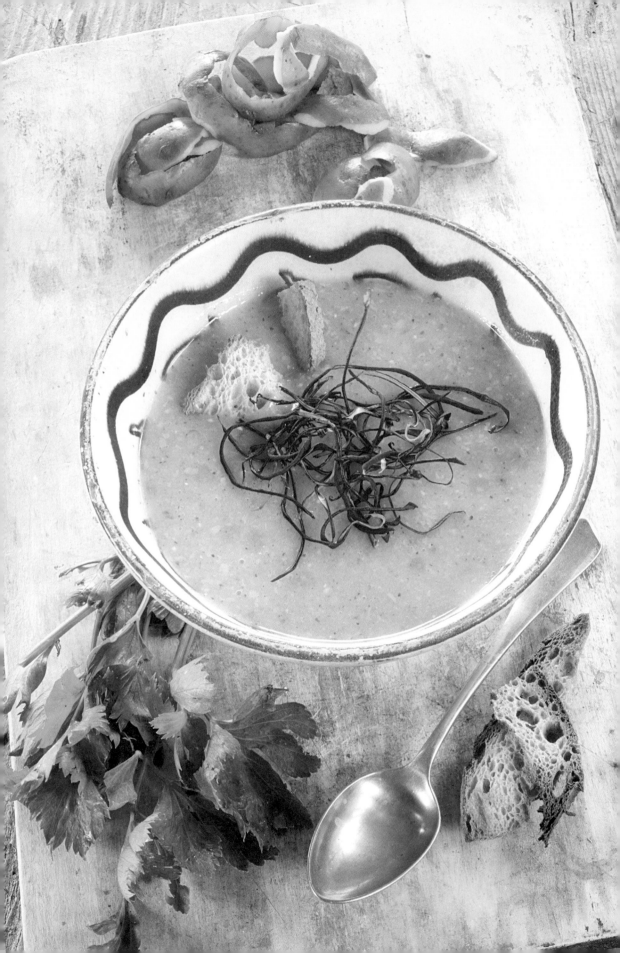

CREAM OF ASPARAGUS ENDS SOUP

4

Easy

10 minutes

55 minutes

- 20 asparagus spears (the hard, white part)
- 2 white potatoes, peeled and diced
- 4 dried onion leaves
- 4 pieces of dried celery
- 1 tbsp dried leek leaves
- 1 1/2 tbsp (20 g) butter
- 2 tsp (5 g) corn flour
- chives
- salt and pepper

Make the vegetable broth by boiling 4 1/4 cups (1 l) of water with the onion leaves, celery, leek leaves, and salt and pepper to taste. Boil for 20 minutes, and then strain.

Wash the asparagus spears, remove any parts that have turned brown due to oxidation, and cut them into rounds or sticks. Boil them in the vegetable broth with the diced potatoes. If you also want to use the potato skins, be aware that they will give the soup a darker color.

Boil for 30 minutes, reducing the broth by about half, then blend thoroughly. Whisk in the butter and corn flour, and continue to cook for another 2–3 minutes. Season with salt and pepper to taste.

Finally, sprinkle with freshly cut chives.

CREAMY ARTICHOKE LEAF SOUP

2

Easy

10 minutes

40 minutes

- the outer leaves of 2 artichokes
- 1 onion
- 1 potato
- 4 1/2 tbsp (30 g) Parmigiano Reggiano shavings
- 1 slice of stale bread
- 2 tbsp extra virgin olive oil
- 2 tbsp white vinegar
- salt and pepper

Fill a saucepan with 4 1/4 cups (1 l) of water and add the vinegar. Remove the petals of the artichokes, and put them in the water one by one. If there are thorns on the ends of the petals, cut them off.

Wash and slice the onion, then peel and dice the potato. Add these to the water, cover with a lid, and leave to boil over low heat. Check to see if the petals are cooked after 30 minutes: they should fall apart to the touch. Season with salt and pepper, and then blend.

Leave the soup to cook for a further 10 minutes, without the lid, until it thickens. If necessary, add more salt and pepper.

If you want it even thicker, you can cook the soup over high heat, or add 1 tsp of corn flour or starch.

Serve the soup piping hot, with stale bread, a drizzle of oil, and the Parmigiano Reggiano shavings.

CORN STOCK WITH CELERY LEAVES AND SPRING ONION

2

Easy

5 minutes

1 hour

- the leaves of 1 ear of corn
- 1 corncob
- 1 spring onion stalk
- 2 dried celery stalks
- salt and pepper

Wash the fresh ingredients; coarsely chop the corn husks, and cut the spring onion stalk into rounds. Put them in a saucepan with 4 1/4 cups (1 l) of cold water.

Break the corncob in half, or into several pieces, and add it to the other ingredients together with the coarsely crumbled celery.

Boil over low heat for 1 hour, with the lid on, adding salt and pepper if necessary. Strain the broth and use it in risottos, broth-based soups, and hot infusions, or as an appetizer to get the stomach ready for food.

CORN HUSK PARCELS FILLED
WITH POTATO, EGGPLANT, AND PARSLEY

4

Easy

15 minutes

20 minutes

10 minutes

- the skins of 2 potatoes
- 1/4 cup (50 g) millet
- 2 tbsp dried tomato and eggplant skins
- the skin of 1 red onion
- 10 dried parsley stalks
- 7 oz (200 g) finely chopped tofu
- 16 green corn husks
- 4 tbsp extra virgin olive oil
- salt and pepper
- kitchen twine or string

For this recipe, use only the skins of fresh or well-preserved potatoes, free of shoots and green spots, and with a smooth surface. Wash them, and then cook them in 2 1/4 cups (1/2 l) of water over low heat, with the lid on, together with the millet, salt, and pepper.

Drain them after 20 minutes, then add the tomato, eggplant, and onion skins, and finally the parsley. Blend all the ingredients.

Pour the mixture into a bowl, add the tofu, and season with salt and pepper.

Put a tablespoon of the filling onto each of the corn husks, then fold them into parcels and secure them with kitchen string.

Preheat the oven to 425°F (220°C). Brush the parcels with oil, and place them on a baking tray lined with parchment paper.

Cook for 5 minutes on each side. Once cooked, arrange the parcels on a serving plate.

ASPARAGUS ENDS OMELET

4

Easy

15 minutes

10 minutes

- 10 asparagus spears (the hard, white part)
- 4 eggs
- 4 1/2 tbsp (30 g) grated Parmigiano Reggiano
- 1 tbsp dried tomato skins
- 3 1/2 oz (100 g) mixed salad, washed and dried
- 2 tbsp olive oil
- salt and pepper

Wash the asparagus spears and cut them into rounds or strips.

Cook over low heat with 1 tbsp of oil, adding a few tablespoons of water so that they don't burn. Remove from heat after about 10 minutes, drain off any remaining water, and finely chop using a mezzaluna or food processor.

Pour the mixture into a bowl, add the eggs, Parmigiano Reggiano, salt and pepper to taste, and then stir.

Pour the remaining oil into a non-stick frying pan and heat. When hot, add the mixture and cook over low heat with the lid on, for about 5 minutes each side.

Place the tomato skins in a mortar, and grind them with a pestle.

Put the salad on a serving plate, put the omelet in the middle, and sprinkle with the ground tomato skins.

SLICED BROCCOLI STEMS
WITH GARLIC AND CHILI PEPPER

4

Easy

10 minutes

10 minutes

- 4 broccoli stems with leaves
- 2 garlic cloves
- 2 dried chili peppers
- 1 tsp ground dried tomato skins
- 2 tbsp extra virgin olive oil
- salt

Trim the broccoli stems and cut them into thin strips. Pour the oil into a non-stick frying pan, together with the garlic and chili pepper.

Once the garlic has browned, add the broccoli stems and a little water, stir, and cook for about 10 minutes. Continue adding a splash of water every now and then — the stems should be stewed, not boiled.

Add salt to taste, check that the stems are the desired consistency, then add the ground tomato skins. Take off the heat and serve.

OIL FLAVORED WITH DRIED VEGETABLES AND SPICES

34 fl oz (1 l)

Easy

10 minutes

1 day

- 34 fl oz (1 l) oil in a bottle
- 10 green garlic and spring onion leaves
- 1 tbsp dried tomato skins
- 1 tbsp dried celery
- 1 tbsp chopped leftover bell pepper
- 6 dried carrot tops
- 1 tsp mustard seeds
- 1 tsp cardamom
- 1 tsp pepper

1 hour

Sun-dry the garlic and spring onion leaves, leaving them in the sun for one day, and turning them over regularly.

If you prefer to dry them in the oven, heat to 100–120°F (40–50°C) and leave them to dry for about an hour, with the oven door slightly open.

Put all of the ingredients into the bottle of oil; leave to rest for a couple of days, shaking the bottle every now and then.

Use the flavored oil for flavoring salads, soups, sauces, and condiments. To fully appreciate its subtle aromas, the oil is best used cold.

MIXED SALAD DRESSED
WITH AROMATIC OIL AND SEEDS

2

Easy

5 minutes

- 5 oz (150 g) different vegetable leaves: turnip, carrot, chard, etc.
- 1 tbsp mixed pumpkin and melon seeds
- 2 tbsp oil flavored with tomato skins, celery, fennel, onion, and spices
- unrefined salt

Toast the seeds in a non-stick frying pan. Leave to cool for about 1 minute, finely chop them, and add the unrefined salt.

Trim the vegetable leaves, and gently dry them by patting them with a piece of paper towel. Put them into a salad bowl, dress with flavored oil, sprinkle with seeds, mix, and serve.

CELERIAC SALAD WITH FLAVORED OIL AND DRIED VEGETABLES

2

Easy

10 minutes

5 minutes

- 7 oz (200 g) celeriac
- 2 handfuls of mixed dried vegetable ribbons
- 2 tbsp oil, flavored with dried vegetables and spices
- orange flavored salt *(see recipe on p. 138)*

Wash the celeriac thoroughly, scrub the skin, then cut into thin slices using a mandoline or a meat slicer.

Roast the vegetables in the oven at 400°F (200°C) for 5 minutes, until they are crispy and crunchy. You can add a little salt if you like.

Arrange the celeriac on a serving plate, season with orange flavored salt, and dress with flavored oil. Add the vegetables at the last minute, as they will lose their crispiness the moment they come into contact with the celeriac and oil.

Protein-Based Recipes

It might seem like a gamble to make stock with shrimp shells and fish heads, but when you sip that tasty tablespoonful when it's ready, all your doubts will be dispelled! So, after having filleted a fish, don't throw away the scraps: put everything in a pot, together with some aromatic herbs, garlic, and lemon peel, and when the stock's ready you can make an amazing risotto.

This advice also applies to the crusts of some types of cheese, such as Parmigiano Reggiano, which is naturally free of preservatives. A small piece of crust added to the stock gives it a wonderful aroma and flavor.

In general, you can use the scraps of anything to create surprisingly good dishes: for example, with the scraps of the vegetables used for making juices, you can make scrumptious medallions coated in crunchy flour made with pumpkin seeds and skins, or a delicious soup with the hard petals of artichokes. As our grandmothers used to tell us, leftovers can be turned into new dishes that can taste even better!

And let's not forget salmon skin. Here we can learn from the Japanese culinary tradition of transforming many types of grilled fish skins into delicious rolls. Just remove the scales from the skin, and leave it under the grill for a few minutes, to create a delicious and original dish that will amaze with its intense flavor and wonderful texture. For a healthy, balanced, and nutritious result, you must always buy foods that have not been treated with preservatives.

CHEESE BALLS
WITH GARDEN HERBS

2

Easy

20 minutes

- 7 oz (200 g) hard and soft cheese leftovers
- 5 dried carrot tops
- 2 tbsp dried tomato skins
- 10 dried spring onion leaves
- 1 tbsp dried bell pepper scraps

Finely chop the dried vegetables and herbs using a food processor or a mortar and pestle.

Once you have a uniform consistency, put the mixture on a piece of food grade paper.

Chop the leftover cheeses, then mix them until you have a smooth mixture. Make small balls, and then roll them in the vegetable coating.

Arrange the balls on a serving plate, and leave them in the fridge until you are ready to serve them.

They make a delicious accompaniment to an aperitif or a really tasty appetizer.

JERUSALEM ARTICHOKE SKINS AND ANCHOVIES WITH BELL PEPPERS

4

Easy

10 minutes

25 minutes

- 7 oz (200 g) Jerusalem artichoke skins
- 8 salt-packed anchovies
- 1 peeled garlic clove
- 8 bell pepper quarters, trimmed and washed
- 2 tbsp extra virgin olive oil
- 1/2 cup (1 dl) white wine vinegar
- salt and pepper

Trim the Jerusalem artichoke skins and steam them for about 20 minutes, until they are soft; then leave them to dry.

Wash the anchovies, remove the spine, and dry them.

Finely chop them together with the Jerusalem artichoke skins and the garlic clove; season with oil and pepper.

Boil the bell pepper quarters in salted water together with the vinegar; check their consistency after 7 minutes (they mustn't be too soft because they have to maintain their shape). Drain and leave them to cool. Fill them with the Jerusalem artichoke and anchovy mixture, and serve.

SHRIMP STOCK

2

Easy

5 minutes

40 minutes

- 10 shrimp heads and shells
- 1 tbsp dried leek scraps
- 2 pieces of lemon peel
- 1 garlic clove
- the skin of 1 onion
- 1 bunch of dried parsley stalks
- 1 tsp finely chopped carrot tops
- lemon flavored salt *(see recipe on p. 138)*
- pepper

Boil the shrimp heads and shells in 4 1/4 cups (1 l) of water, then add the dried leek, lemon peel, garlic, onion, and the bunch of parsley.

Cook for about 30 minutes, with the lid on.

Strain and boil for a further 10 minutes over high heat, without the lid, to reduce the stock.

Season with salt and pepper to taste.

Before serving, sprinkle with the chopped carrot tops.

The stock can be used to make sauces and soups, or served on its own. You can also use the leftovers to make risottos.

CREAMY CARDOON LEAF STEM MILK SOUP

4

Easy

10 minutes

- 1 center core of a cardoon
- 1 white potato
- 2 1/4 cups (1/2 l) milk
- salt and pepper

30 minutes

The center core of a cardoon is composed of leaf stems, the consistency of which makes them difficult to eat, but if you boil them in milk, they soften and lose most of their bitter taste.

Wash the cardoon leaf stems and the potato; coarsely chop the vegetables and boil them in the milk, diluted with 2 1/4 cups (1/2 l) of water.

Leave to cook over low heat for about 30 minutes, then blend until creamy.

Season with salt and pepper to taste.

This soup is dedicated to those who love bitter foods. If you want to sweeten it, add a tablespoon of cream cheese or mascarpone.

FISH BROTH WITH RED RICE

4

Easy

10 minutes

1 hour

- the heads and bones of 2 small fish (or 1 large one)
- 2 garlic shoots
- 3/4 cup (150 g) red rice
- 8 dried onion leaves
- 1 tsp chopped parsley
- 2 tbsp extra virgin olive oil
- orange flavored salt *(see recipe on p. 138)*
- pepper

Wash the garlic shoots.

Boil the fish scraps in 4 1/4 cups (1 l) of water with 1 garlic shoot, complete with roots, slicing the green parts into rounds (put a little bit to one side).

Leave to cook over low heat for about 30 minutes, with the lid on. Drain, collect the fleshy parts, crumble them, and put them back in the broth.

Put the red rice in a pan with water, cook for 10 minutes, then drain. Pour the oil into a frying pan, and add the remaining sliced garlic. Cook for 1 minute, then add the rice and continue cooking, adding the broth a little at a time when necessary.

Stir regularly; season with salt and pepper to taste.

When the rice reaches the desired consistency (red rice cooks in about 30 minutes), remove from heat, decorate with pieces of onion leaf, sprinkle with parsley, and serve.

RICE SOUP WITH PARMIGIANO REGGIANO CRUSTS

4

Easy

5 minutes

1 hour

- 1/2 cup (100 g) brown rice
- 1 garlic shoot
- 2 tbsp dried leek
- 1 tbsp dried celery
- 4 pieces of Parmigiano Reggiano crust (about 14 oz or 40 g)
- 2 tbsp extra virgin olive oil
- salt and pepper

Trim the garlic shoot, and cut it into rounds; put them into a pan containing 6 1/4 cups (1 1/2 l) of water, add the leek, celery, and brown rice, and bring to a boil.

Scrape the Parmigiano Reggiano crusts with a knife, wash them, and add to the soup.

Season with salt and pepper to taste during cooking. Leave to boil until the crusts are soft and the rice almost falls apart to the touch (it should take about 60 minutes).

Serve piping hot, with a drizzle of cold olive oil.

GREEN PEA PASTA WITH DRIED ASPARAGUS, PARSLEY, AND CARROT SCRAPS

2

Easy

5 minutes

10 minutes

- 6 oz (160 g) green pea pasta
- 2 oz (50 g) mixed cheese leftovers
- 2 tbsp dried parsley, asparagus spear scraps, carrot skins
- 2 tsp finely chopped pumpkin flesh and seeds, salted
- 4 dried carrot tops
- 4 dried spring onion leaves
- 2 tbsp of butter

Grate the cheeses and melt them in a pan with the butter.

Chop the parsley, carrot skins, and asparagus spears, and fold them into the cheese.

Boil the pasta in plenty of salted water.

Follow the cooking times on the packet. When it reaches the desired consistency, drain and pour it into the cheese sauce.

Put the pasta on the plates, and sprinkle the chopped pumpkin flesh and seeds on top, which will add a touch of delicious crunchiness.

Finally, crumble the carrot tops on top, and decorate with spring onion leaves.

TROFIE WITH CARROT TOP PESTO

4

Easy

10 minutes

10 minutes

- 12 oz (350 g) fresh trofie
- 10 fresh carrot tops
- 4 sprigs of basil
- 1 garlic clove
- 2 oz (50 g) grated Parmigiano Reggiano
- 1 oz (30 g) peeled hazelnuts
- 5 tbsp extra virgin olive oil
- salt and pepper

Trim the carrot tops and sprigs of basil, and put them in a mortar or on a wooden chopping board. Peel the garlic and add it to the herbs. Finely chop the hazelnuts.

Either use a pestle to grind the herbs and garlic, or a mezzaluna to finely chop them, then add them to the hazelnuts; add the Parmigiano Reggiano and olive oil. Season with salt and pepper, and mix until the mixture is creamy.

Boil the trofie in plenty of salted water. When it reaches the desired consistency, drain and add the pasta to the sauce. Transfer to a serving dish.

Serve piping hot.

RAVIOLI WITH ARTICHOKE SCRAPS
AND MATURE RICOTTA

4

Easy

60 minutes

3–4 minutes

- the scraps of 2 artichokes
- 2 cups (200 g) all-purpose flour
- 2 eggs
- 2 yolks
- 1 boiled potato
- 2 oz (50 g) grated Parmigiano Reggiano
- 2 oz (50 g) mature ricotta
- 3 tbsp (40 g) butter
- 2 tbsp extra virgin olive oil
- salt and pepper

Trim the artichoke leaves and remove the thorns. Pour the oil into a frying pan, and simmer the leaves until soft. Blend and divide the mixture into two parts: one part for the sauce, and one for the filling. Pour about 4/5 of the artichokes into a bowl, add 1 yolk, the grated Parmigiano Reggiano, and the potato, mashed thoroughly. Season with salt and pepper to taste, mix the ingredients thoroughly, and put into a pastry bag.

Make the pasta by mixing the remaining eggs with the flour, adding a few tablespoons of water if necessary.

Knead vigorously, and when the dough is smooth, shiny, and lump-free, roll it out thinly with a rolling pin. Then, using a pastry wheel or a cookie cutter, make the ravioli (or create any shape you like), and fill them with the artichoke mixture.

Make the sauce by mixing the remaining artichoke mixture, the butter, and 1 tbsp of grated ricotta.

Boil the ravioli in salted water. When they reach the desired consistency (3–4 minutes is long enough), drain, pour them into the sauce, add a freshly cut slice of ricotta, and serve.

CHEESE AND DRIED VEGETABLE CREPES

2

Medium

15 minutes

10 minutes

5 minutes

For the crepes:
- 3/4 cup (2 dl) milk
- 2 eggs
- 1/2 cup (60 g) corn flour
- 1 1/2 tbsp (20 g) olive oil

For the sauce:
- 1 tbsp mixed dried skins: bell pepper, tomato, and cucumber
- 1 tbsp finely chopped pumpkin skin and seeds, and mustard seeds
- 9 oz (250 g) ready-made bechamel sauce
- 3 1/2 oz (100 g) chopped fontina cheese
- salt and pepper

To make the crepes, mix the milk, eggs, and corn flour in a bowl until the batter is smooth and lump-free. Dip a little bit of paper towel in oil, and grease the bottom and edges of a non-stick frying pan with a diameter of about 8 in (20 cm). Cover the bottom of the pan with a thin, even layer of batter, and as soon as it sets, turn it over and cook for a few more seconds.

Remove from the heat when the crepe starts sliding and releases easily from the frying pan. Repeat until you have finished all the batter. Put the crepes to one side until you need them.

Grind the bell pepper and tomato skins together; break the cucumber peel into pieces. Fill each crepe with a little bechamel sauce, a few pieces of cheese, a pinch of ground bell pepper and tomato skins, and a few bits of cucumber. Divide the crepes between two baking trays, season with the chopped pumpkin scraps, the ground bell pepper and tomato skins, and bits of cucumber. Season with salt and pepper to taste as you are preparing the crepes.

Heat in the oven for 5 minutes at 425°F (220°C), and then serve.

TOFU WITH EGGPLANT AND VEGETABLES

2

Easy

10 minutes

10 minutes

- 7 oz (200 g) tofu
- 7 oz (200 g) eggplant
- 1 garlic shoot
- 1 tbsp dried celery leaves
- 1 tbsp dried tomato skins
- 1 tbsp dried bell pepper scraps
- 3 1/2 oz (100 g) non-dairy cream
- 1/4 cup (0.5 dl) peanut oil
- salt

Preheat the oven to 400°F (200°C). Slice the eggplant.
Heat the oil, and fry the slices of eggplant a few at a time.

When they're cooked, drain them and put them on a paper towel.

Finely slice the green part of the garlic shoot. Chop the dried
vegetables together, putting a few tomato skins to one side
for decorating the dish.

Finely slice the tofu.

Using two individual baking dishes, create alternate layers of slices
of eggplant and tofu; season with the chopped vegetables, salt,
and half the garlic shoot, then add the non-dairy cream.

Cook in the oven for 10 minutes. Before serving, decorate
with pieces of tomato skin and the remaining garlic.

CARROT AND BROCCOLI BALLS

2

Easy

10 minutes

10 minutes

- solid carrot and broccoli leftovers
- 3 1/2 oz (100 g) grated Parmigiano Reggiano
- 1 oz (30 g) flour made with pumpkin and melon seeds, and dried pumpkin and carrot skins
- salt

For the coating:
- 3 1/2 oz (100 g) flour made with pumpkin and melon seeds, and dried pumpkin and melon skins
- 1/2 cup (1 dl) sesame oil

Put the carrot and broccoli scraps in a bowl, add the Parmigiano Reggiano, seed flour, and salt, then mix thoroughly.

Make the balls the size you want them, and then roll them in the flour for the coating.

Heat the sesame oil, and fry the balls for about 10 minutes, making sure they are golden brown on all sides. When they are nice and crunchy, remove from the heat, and drain on a paper towel.

PEAR, FIG, APPLE, AND PUMPKIN MUSTARD SERVED WITH CHEESE

4

Easy

15 minutes

- 2 whole pears
- 3 1/2 oz (100 g) pumpkin with the skin
- 2 oz (50 g) dried fig skins
- 30 pieces of dried apple peel
- 1 oz (20 g) melon rind
- 1 tbsp mustard seeds
- 1/2 cup (100 g) sugar
- 1 tbsp apple vinegar

1 hour

Wash the pears and cut into pieces.

Trim the pumpkin, then dice the flesh and skin separately.
Put all the fruit and skins (figs, apples, melon) in a pan,
together with the sugar, mustard seeds, and vinegar.

Mix, and leave to cook over low heat for about 1 hour.

The mixture should thicken and reduce by about 1/3. Once cooked,
make sure it is completely amalgamated, and transfer to a container.

Before serving, arrange the cheeses you have chosen to serve
with the mustard on a platter (slightly piquant cheeses are best).

CRISPY SALMON SKIN WITH RICE

2

Easy

5 minutes

- 1/4 cup (50 g) white rice
- 6 pieces of salmon skin
- 1 tbsp (10 g) dried cucumber peel
- 2 tbsp extra virgin olive oil
- salt

20 minutes

8 minutes

Add double the volume of water to the rice, and bring to a boil.

Cook with the lid on, and take off the heat when the rice has absorbed all of the water. Add the oil and salt to taste, then put to one side until you are ready to use it.

Remove any scales from the salmon skin, then wash and dry it. Arrange the skins on a baking tray.

Preheat the oven to 400°F (200°C). Put in the oven and turn on the grill so that the skins cook quickly and become crispy.

Turn them over regularly, and take them out of the oven after about 8 minutes.

Press the rice into small containers, then turn out onto serving plates. Add the salmon skin and the cucumber peel, then serve.

Fruit-Based Recipes

The continuous research and studies on fruit skins and their well-known properties — not to mention their unexpected ones — verify what perhaps our grandmothers already knew: that fruit skins are a treasure trove of nutrients that we should take full advantage of. We must be less trusting, however, when buying fruit: we should always be suspicious of a beautiful piece of fruit without any imperfections, with a perfect size and color, and similar-looking to all those around it. It is rare for a plant to produce perfect fruit that all look the same, so it is preferable that there are some defects to prove the naturalness of the product. A fruit's smell is essential to establishing its freshness: if it is intense, it means that the fruit is ripe, ready to be eaten, and that it has not been kept in the refrigerator for a long time! If you buy organic products, building a relationship of trust with the producer or store, it will be easier for you to be sure you are buying healthy fruit. Another way of determining a fruit's goodness and naturalness is finding out if it is in season. Locally grown seasonal fruit will rarely contain preservatives and will have been picked while unripe. Fruit that have a long way to travel from their place of origin to our local stores, on the other hand, will undergo specific treatments to slow down ripening and preserve their freshness until they are sold. Finally, in addition to being an ethical decision, using all parts of a fruit is undoubtedly beneficial to our health and well-being. This section contains simple recipes that use fruit peels and rinds, with original combinations that will amaze your guests.

SNACK WITH MELON AND PUMPKIN RINDS AND SEEDS

4

Easy

10 minutes

10 minutes

- 3 1/2 oz (100 g) mixed dried seeds and pumpkin and melon rinds
- 1 1/2 cups (200 g) whole-wheat flour
- 1/2 cup (100 g) peanut oil
- salt

Finely chop the rinds and seeds. Stir them into the flour, and mix with about 1/2 cup (1 dl) of water, added a little at a time.

Once you have obtained a smooth dough, roll it out thinly with a rolling pin (the dough should be no more than 0.04 in or 1 mm thick). Cut into rectangles or strips, or whatever shape you like. Score the surface so that they are crispy when cooked.

Heat the oil, and fry the rinds a few at a time, until you have cooked them all. Drain, place on a piece of paper towel, and sprinkle with salt.

POTATO SKIN AND MELON SEED BREAD

4

Medium

15 minutes

30 minutes

- 1 1/2 cups (200 g) whole-wheat flour
- the skins of 4 boiled potatoes
- 1 tbsp sesame seeds
- 2 tbsp melon seeds
- 4 pieces of dried melon rind
- 2 tsp (5 g) baker's yeast
- 2 tbsp olive oil
- salt

Finely chop the potato skins and put them in a bowl.

Chop the sesame seeds, melon seeds, and the dried melon rind (put a few whole melon seeds to one side for decorating).

Stir the flour into the potato mixture and add the chopped seeds. Dissolve the yeast in 1/2 cup (1 dl) of warm water, and add it to the mixture.

Knead until you obtain a smooth, lump-free dough, and leave it to rise for 30 minutes.

Divide the dough into two equal portions, roll into small sausage shapes, and put them in the molds, previously greased with olive oil.

Decorate the loaves with the remaining seeds, and bake for 30 minutes at 350°F (180°C). Insert a toothpick into the center of the bread to see if it is cooked: if it comes out dry and clean, you can take the bread out of the oven.

DRIED APPLE PEEL

Easy

10 minutes

1 day

1 hour

• 4 red and green apples

Apple peel is often discarded when making cakes, but you can dry it, and use it to make other things.

Wash the apples thoroughly, remove the peel, and place it on a piece of parchment paper. If the season allows, leave it to dry in the sun for a whole day.

On a sunny winter's day, you can leave them to dry on a windowsill, or put them in the oven at low temperature for about 1 hour: it must be no hotter than 120°F (50°C), and the over door must be left slightly open.

Turn the peels over regularly, and take them out of the oven when they are completely dry.

Store them in a jar, and use them dried or rehydrated in water, or finely chopped to enrich cookies and cakes.

DRIED PEAR SKINS

Easy

10 minutes

2 days

• 2 pears

Pear skins are a little more difficult because ripe pears are very juicy and high in water. This means they need longer to dry than other fruit and vegetables.

Wash and peel the pears, and place the skins on a piece of paper towel. Gently dab them with a tea towel, and then arrange them on a piece of parchment paper.

Put them in the sun, and leave them to dry for 2 days, covering them at night so they don't get damp. Turn them over regularly; when they are firm and dry, you can put them in a jar. The skins can be used dried, ground, or rehydrated.

If you use a food dehydrator, follow the manufacturer's instructions.

SWEET SNACKS

4

Easy

- 4 apples
- 4 peaches
- 2 bananas
- 10 figs

20 minutes

1 day

2 hours

Wash the apples, remove the peels, and place them on a piece of parchment paper. Leave them to dry in the sun (a day is usually enough for them to dry completely), and then put them in a glass jar.

Wash the peaches, and then rub the skins vigorously to remove the fuzz. You can sun-dry the skins, or put them in the oven at 120°F (50°C), with the door slightly open, for about 2 hours, turning them over regularly.

Wash, dry, and peel the bananas, and then cut the skins into thin strips. You can either dry them in a food dehydrator, following the times indicated in the instructions, or dry them in the sun.

Peel the figs, and put the skins on a piece of parchment paper. Leave them in the sun for a whole day, turning them regularly.

Serve the dried fruit skins as a delicious snack, or as original nibbles to go with an aperitif.

FRUIT AND ALMOND BUNS

4

Easy

15 minutes

- 1 oz (30 g) mixed dried skins: fig, apple, mango, pear, and peach
- 9 oz (250 g) ready-made puff pastry
- 1/3 cup (30 g) ground almonds
- 2 tbsp (40 g) honey

20 minutes

Roughly break up the dried fruit skins. Put the puff pastry on a work surface, and cut into ribbons about 1 in (2.5 cm) wide.

Divide the dried fruit between the pastry ribbons, and then roll each one up.

Preheat the oven to 350°F (180°C), and line a baking tray with parchment paper.

Pour the ground almonds onto a plate, brush the rolls with honey, and then coat them with almonds.

Put the rolls on the baking tray, and bake for 20 minutes, checking every now and then that they aren't burning.

CHOCOLATE, FIG, AND ORANGE COOKIES

4

Medium

15 minutes

- 3/4 cup (100 g) whole-wheat flour
- 1 oz (30 g) fig skins
- the dried rind of half an orange
- 1 oz (30 g) dark chocolate
- 2 egg yolks
- 3 1/2 tbsp (50 g) butter
- 1/3 cup (50 g) brown sugar

For decorating: 2 1/4 tbsp (20 g) brown sugar

15 minutes

Melt the butter over a bain-marie. Finely chop the fig skins, putting aside a few pieces for decorating. Finely chop half of the orange rind, and put the other half to one side.

Put the flour, chopped fig and orange, sugar, melted butter, and yolks into a bowl, and stir until the mixture is smooth.

Line a baking tray with parchment paper, and preheat the oven to 350°F (180°C). Melt the chocolate over a bain-marie, then keep it warm until you need it.

Roll the dough out to a thickness of 0.2 in (1/2 cm) with a rolling pin, cut into geometric shapes, and put them on a baking tray. Bake for 15 minutes, remove from the oven, and leave to cool for a few minutes.

Decorate the warm cookies with a few pieces of fig skin, 1 tsp of chocolate, sugar, and the remaining orange rind, cut into small pieces. Leave to cool, and serve.

PEAR AND MANGO SKIN COOKIES WITH CHOCOLATE AND HONEY

4

Medium

15 minutes

15 minutes

- 2 cups (200 g) all-purpose flour
- the dried skin of 1 mango
- the dried skin of 2 pears
- 2 egg yolks
- 3 1/2 tbsp (50 g) butter
- 3 tbsp (60 g) wildflower honey
- 3 1/2 oz (100 g) dark chocolate

Preheat the oven to 400°F (200°C). Finely chop the fruit skins in a food processor.

Melt the chocolate over a bain-marie.

Pour the flour into a bowl, add the butter, 4/5 of the honey, yolks, and the chopped skins. Mix thoroughly, and then with your hands form the dough into a ball. Roll the dough out with a rolling pin.

Cut into rectangles, and place them on a baking tray lined with parchment paper.

Mix the chocolate with the remaining honey, then keep the mixture warm so it doesn't harden.

Bake the cookies for 15 minutes. Check that they are cooking evenly after 10 minutes, and turn them over.

Remove from the oven, drizzle with the honey chocolate, and leave to cool.

PEACH SKIN COOKIES

4

Medium

20 minutes

17 minutes

- 1 1/2 cups (200 g) whole-wheat flour
- the dried skins of 3 peaches
- 1 egg yolk
- 1/4 cup (50 g) granulated sugar
- 1.8 fl oz (50 g) butter melted over a bain-marie
- 2 tsp (5 g) cake yeast
- 0.8 oz (20 g) white chocolate

For decorating: 1 tbsp granulated sugar

Finely chop the peach skins, putting aside about 1/5 for decorating.

Mix the yolk with the sugar, then add all the other ingredients apart from the white chocolate.

Preheat the oven to 350°F (180°C).

Knead the dough thoroughly until it is soft. Make little balls, cut them in half, and place them on a baking tray lined with parchment paper. Bake for 15 minutes.

Cut the chocolate into the same number of pieces as the number of cookies, and do the same with the remaining peach skins.

Take the cookies out of the oven, decorate with a sprinkling of sugar, pieces of chocolate, and peach skins. Put back in the oven for a few minutes, and then leave to cool before serving.

MELON AND LEMON RIND COOKIES

4

Easy

10 minutes

15 minutes

- 2 cups (200 g) all-purpose flour
- 3 egg yolks
- 1/4 cup (50 g) castor sugar
- 1 1/2 tbsp (20 g) soft butter
- 1 oz (30 g) chopped melon rind
- 1 tsp chopped lemon peel
- 1 3/4 oz (50 g) almonds
- 2/3 tsp (2 g) cake yeast

Mix all the ingredients except for the almonds.
When the dough is thoroughly mixed, knead in the almonds.

Preheat the oven to 400°F (200°C).

Divide the dough and make long rolls, about 1 in (2.5 cm) wide, and place them on a baking tray lined with parchment paper.

Leave them to bake for about 15 minutes, remove from the oven, cut into equal-sized slices while still soft, and leave to cool at room temperature.

GRAPEFRUIT AND CHOCOLATE MUFFINS

6

Medium

15 minutes

25 minutes

- 2 cups (200 g) all-purpose flour
- 1/2 cup (100 g) granulated sugar
- 2 eggs
- 1.8 fl oz (50 g) butter melted over a bain-marie
- 1/2 cup (1 dl) milk
- 2/3 tsp (2 g) cake yeast
- 1 oz (30 g) chopped banana skin
- 4 pieces of candied grapefruit peel *(see recipe on p. 132)*
- 10 pieces of fig skin
- 1 oz (30 g) bitter chocolate, pieces or shavings
- 3 tsp sliced almonds

Get two bowls, and in each one put half of the flour and sugar, 1 egg, and half of the butter, yeast, and milk. Add the banana skins to one of the bowls, and half of the grapefruit peel to the other.

Mix both of the mixtures, then line 6 muffin molds with parchment paper.

Preheat the oven to 325°F (170°C).

Pour the mixtures into the molds, filling them to about 2/3. Decorate the top of the banana muffins with chocolate shavings and pieces of fig skin, and the grapefruit muffins with sliced almonds and the remaining grapefruit peel.

Bake for about 25–30 minutes, remove from the oven, and leave to cool.

APPLE PEEL CAKE

4

Medium

10 minutes

- 2 cups (200 g) cake flour
- the skins of 4 apples
- 2 eggs
- 1/4 cup (50 g) granulated sugar
- 1.8 fl oz (50 g) butter melted over a bain-marie
- 2 tsp (5 g) cake yeast

30–40 minutes

Chop half of the apple skins.

Beat the egg whites until stiff. In a bowl, whisk the yolks with the sugar, then stir in the flour, butter, yeast, and chopped skins. Mix thoroughly.

Preheat the oven to 350°F (180°C).

Once the mixture is thoroughly mixed, add the egg whites, and transfer to a high-edged baking tray lined with parchment paper.

Decorate the top with the whole apple skins, and bake for 30 minutes. Insert a toothpick into the center of the cake to see if it is cooked: if it isn't clean, cook for another 10 minutes.

Remove from the oven, and leave to cool before serving.

CANDIED GRAPEFRUIT PEEL

18 oz (500 g)

Easy

10 minutes

40 minutes

- 4 pink grapefruits
- 1 1/2 cups (200 g) brown sugar

Wash the fruit and remove the skin from the pith (the white part) and the segments.

If the grapefruit has been squeezed (and therefore you have two halves), use a tablespoon to scoop out the bits left on the skin.

If there are also pieces of fruit leftover after squeezing, remove the pith and put them in a pan with 4 1/4 cups (1 l) of water together with the skins.

Leave to boil for 20 minutes, put them in another pan with 1/4 of the cooking water, add the sugar, and cook for 15–20 minutes, stirring continuously.

Remove from the heat, leave to cool, and then pour the entire contents of the pan into a jar.

MELON AND LEMON RIND JELLY

14 oz (400 g)

Easy

- 1 melon
- 2 lemons
- 1/2 cup (100 g) granulated sugar
- 2 tsp (5 g) agar-agar (optional)

15 minutes

90 minutes

Wash the melon thoroughly, scrub the rind, and remove the flesh surrounding the seeds. Wash the lemons, cut off the rinds, and chop into small pieces.

Boil the rinds, flesh, and seeds for 30 minutes in 10 1/2 cups (2.5 l) of water.

Cook over medium heat until the water has reduced by 2/3, then add the sugar and continue to boil.

When the mixture is thick and soft (after about 60 minutes), remove from the heat and pour into a jar.

If you like your jelly really thick, you can add the agar-agar 5 minutes before the end of the cooking time; this will thicken the liquid, which then coats the solid parts and binds the jelly.

PIQUANT WATERMELON RIND COMPOTE WITH SPICES

4

Medium

15 minutes

1 hour

- 35 oz (1 kg) watermelon rind
- 1 cup (200 g) granulated sugar
- 1 tbsp coriander seeds
- 1/2 tbsp cardamom seeds
- 1/2 cup (1 dl) orange juice
- 2 tsp (5 g) agar-agar

Wash the watermelon rind and cut into pieces the size of a small teaspoon. Put them in a pan, and add the sugar, seeds, orange juice, and agar-agar.

Cook over medium-low heat for about 1 hour, stirring regularly.

The outer part of the skin will remain pleasantly crunchy and absorb all of the various aromas, while the agar-agar will slightly thicken the liquid, giving the compote a wonderful consistency.

This compote is particularly delicious with meat, vegetables, and cheese.

LEMON AND ORANGE RIND
FLAVORED SALT

7 oz (200 g)

Medium

- 1 green lemon with 2 leaves
- 1 orange
- 1 cup (200 g) hand-harvested, unrefined fleur de sel

10 minutes

1 day

Peel the citrus fruit, removing as much of the slightly bitter pith (the white part) as possible.

If you make your flavored salt in the summer, put the rinds and leaves on a wooden board (keeping them separate), and leave them in the sun for 1 day, turning them regularly so that they dry evenly. This way they remain unaltered.

Finely chop the rinds separately: the lemon rind with its leaves, followed by the orange rind. Divide the salt between two containers, add the lemon to one, and the orange to the other. Mix thoroughly.

Flavored salt has a very long shelf life; lemon salt is indicated for fish dishes, while orange salt is ideal for salads and meat.

TANGERINE PEEL LIQUEUR

34 fl oz (1 l)

Easy

10 minutes

5 minutes

- 6 tangerines
- 2 cups (1/2 l) pure alcohol
- 2 1/2 cups (500 g) brown sugar

Wash and peel the tangerines. Put the peel in a large jar, add the alcohol, and put the lid on.

Leave the mixture to rest in a dark place for 10 days, then take the peel out of the jar.

Boil 4 1/4 cups (1 l) of water with the sugar for 5 minutes. Remove from the heat, add the tangerine peel, leave to cool, and then strain.

Stir in the alcohol, and then pour the liqueur into bottles. Keep in the refrigerator.

Leftover Bread
or Other Food

Throwing away leftover bread, cooked rice, pasta, or other types of food is

an unjustified waste, as it is very easy to transform them into excellent ingredients

for creating new dishes. Finely ground leftover bread can be used as breading

for meat or vegetable balls, while broken pieces or slices of bread are a perfect base

ingredient for broths, soups, and snacks. Plain cooked rice can be used to thicken

soups and make them smooth and creamy, whereas seasoned rice is ideal

for making croquettes. And what about all those boxes in the cupboard with less

than a handful of pasta left in them? You can pour them all into a pan of boiling

water, one by one — respecting the cooking times indicated on the boxes —

and make a simple, yet imaginative plate of pasta, with lots of different shapes

that children will just love. If you use a mixture of colors and flavors too, it will look

and taste even better! In Italy, for example, it is a long-standing tradition to use

leftovers to make superb dishes, and there is always fresh bread — the basis

of most Italians' diet — on the table at meal times and, consequently, stale leftover

bread in the bread bin! Considering that stale bread appears to be more digestible,

we should include it in our diet and find out just how many ways we can use it.

For a healthy, affordable, and sustainable snack to keep hunger at bay, freshen up

a piece or slice of stale bread in the oven for a few minutes, then serve

with a drizzle of oil and a sprinkle of herbs!

TOMATO AND CHILI PEPPER BREAD

4

Easy

- 7 oz (200 g) stale, but not dry bread
- 1 tbsp dried bell pepper and chili pepper scraps
- 1 tbsp dried tomato skins

10 minutes

6–8 minutes

Thinly slice the bread, using a meat slicer or a very sharp knife.

Finely grind the bell pepper and chili pepper scraps and tomato skins, using a mortar and pestle or a food processor.

Preheat the oven to 400°F (200°C).

Arrange the slices of bread on a baking tray, season with the ground chili pepper, bell pepper, and tomato skins, and toast each side for 3–4 minutes, depending on the thickness of the slices.

Once toasted, put the bread in a bread basket. You can serve it with soup or cheese, or just eat as a tasty snack!

TOFU AND EGGPLANT SKIN SPREAD WITH STALE BREAD CROSTINI

4

Easy

10 minutes

20 minutes

20–25 minutes

- 7 oz (200 g) stale bread
- 1 tsp ground dried tomato skins
- 1/3 oz (10 g) dried eggplant skins
- 3 1/2 oz (100 g) eggplant flesh
- 3 1/2 oz (100 g) tofu
- 1/4 oz (5 g) dried cucumber peel
- 4 tbsp sesame oil
- salt and pepper

Finely chop the eggplant and tomato skins.

Steam the eggplant flesh until soft (it takes about 20 minutes), drain thoroughly, and blend.

Chop the tofu, then add all the other ingredients (including the cucumber peel), apart from the bread, and mix. Season with salt and pepper, add the oil, and pour the spread into a bowl.

Cut the bread into very thin slices, place on a baking tray, season with the ground tomato skins, and toast in the oven at 400°F (200°C) for a few minutes on each side. Put the toasted bread into a bread basket, and serve with the eggplant and tofu spread.

STALE BREAD AND MIXED
DRIED VEGETABLE SOUP

4

Easy

10 minutes

30 minutes

38 minutes

- 1/3 oz (10 g) dried leek leaves
- 3 1/2 oz (100 g) chopped pumpkin flesh and skin
- 1 chopped potato
- 1/4 oz (5 g) dried celery
- 5 dried carrot skins
- 1/4 oz (5 g) dried onion skins
- 2 tbsp flavored oil
- 3 1/2 oz (100 g) sliced stale bread
- salt and pepper

For decorating:
- dried vegetables to taste

Boil all of the ingredients (apart from the bread)
in 4 1/4 cups (1 l) of water.

Season with salt and pepper to taste. Keep the lid on so the liquid
doesn't evaporate. Cook the soup for about 30 minutes,
then blend in a blender.

Slice the bread and place it on a baking tray. Toast in the oven
at 400°F (200°C), 4 minutes for each side.

Divide the toasted bread between the bowls, cover with soup,
decorate with pieces of dried vegetables, and serve piping hot.

LEFTOVER RICE SOUP
WITH TOFU AND EDAMAME

2

Easy

10 minutes

40 minutes

- 3 1/2 oz (100 g) cooked brown rice
- 1 onion
- 7 oz (200 g) edamame
- 3 1/2 oz (100 g) tofu
- 2 tbsp extra virgin olive oil
- 2 tsp finely chopped pumpkin skin and pumpkin and melon seeds, toasted and salted
- salt and pepper

Wash and slice the onion. Put it in a pan with 6 1/4 cups (1 1/2 l) of water, together with the rice.

Trim the edamame and add them to the broth.

Cut the tofu into pieces.

Leave to boil over high heat for 30 minutes, without the lid. Blend, cook for a further 10 minutes, and then add the tofu.

Once cooked, the broth should have reduced by half.

Pour into bowls, add the oil and the chopped pumpkin and melon, season with salt and pepper, and serve.

FANTASY PASTA WITH DRIED VEGETABLE LEFTOVERS

4

Easy

10 minutes

20–25 minutes

- 10 oz (300 g) different types of pasta
- 1 tbsp dried artichoke
- 1 tbsp dried leek
- 1 tbsp grated Parmigiano Reggiano
- 4 tbsp extra virgin olive oil
- salt and pepper

For decorating and seasoning:
- 2 green garlic leaves
- 6 thin strips of eggplant skin

Boil the dried artichoke and leek in salted water for 10 minutes. Drain thoroughly, and blend. Add the oil and Parmigiano Reggiano, and mix.

Bring a large pan of salted water to a boil, add all of the different pastas (start with the one that needs cooking the longest, then add the others one by one according to their cooking times).

Drain the pasta and pour it into the artichoke and leek sauce; season with salt and pepper.

Chop the garlic leaves, stir them into the pasta, slice the eggplant skins, and serve them with the pasta.

SPINACH HAMBURGER WITH SAVOY CABBAGE, RADICCHIO, AND ENDIVE CORES

4

Medium

15 minutes

15 minutes

- 7 oz (200 g) savoy cabbage core
- the cores of 1 radicchio head and 1 endive head
- 2 garlic cloves
- 2 sprigs of rosemary
- 2 tbsp extra virgin olive oil

For the hamburgers:
- 3 1/2 oz (100 g) spinach, cooked and drained
- 2 tbsp dried carrot skins
- 2 dried celery leaves
- 1/4 oz (5 g) dried eggplant and bell pepper skins
- 10 tbsp (50 g) grated Parmigiano Reggiano
- 2 eggs
- 1/2 cup (50 g) breadcrumbs (made with leftover dry bread)
- 1/2 cup (1 dl) peanut oil
- salt and pepper

To make the hamburgers, finely chop the spinach and dried vegetables, and put them into a bowl. Add the cheese and the egg, season with salt and pepper to taste, mix thoroughly, and place on a piece of parchment paper. Level the mixture, and cut out discs with a 3 in (about 8 cm) ring mold. Coat all the hamburgers with breadcrumbs.

Trim the cabbage, radicchio, and endive cores, and put them in a frying pan with the garlic, extra virgin olive oil, and rosemary. Cook over medium heat for 5–7 minutes (depending on the desired consistency). Add salt and pepper during cooking, and stir regularly, adding a tablespoon of water every now and then if necessary.

Fry the hamburgers in very hot peanut oil, cooking each side for about 3 minutes. Transfer them to the frying pan with the vegetables, and serve.

CROQUETTES WITH A DRIED HERB CRUST

2

Easy

10 minutes

10 minutes

- 7 oz (200 g) wild herb leaves and edible flowers
- 2 boiled potatoes with their skins
- 1 egg yolk
- 1 tbsp grated Parmigiano Reggiano
- 1 tbsp mixed dried vegetables: leek, tomato, bell pepper, parsley, garlic, celery, and onion
- 3 1/2 oz (100 g) stale bread
- 1/2 cup (1 dl) sesame oil
- 2 tbsp extra virgin olive oil
- salt and pepper

Trim and wash the wild herb leaves and flowers; leave them to dry on a paper towel. Chop the dry bread and put it on a plate.

Blend the potatoes with their skins in a food processor, add the yolk, cheese, and chopped dried vegetables.

Mix, season with salt and pepper, and form the mixture into patties.

Coat them with breadcrumbs, making sure they stick to the surface. Heat the sesame and olive oil, and when it's really hot (about 338°F or 170°C) add the croquettes.

Make sure they have hardened before turning them over, so as to avoid them falling apart. Fry each side for about 2–3 minutes, and then transfer them to a paper towel.

Arrange the salad on a serving plate, dress with olive oil and salt, and place the croquettes on top.

Index of Ingredients

The Author

CINZIA TRENCHI is a naturopath, freelance journalist, and photographer specializing in nutrition and food and wine. She has contributed to numerous cookbooks, published by both Italian and international publishers. She is a passionate cook, and for many years she has worked with various Italian publications, revisiting regional, traditional, and macrobiotic dishes, providing articles and photographs, as well as her own recipes. Her cookbooks contain original and creative diets, with unusual flavor combinations and pairings for creating new and delicious dishes, always taking into consideration the nutritional composition of foods to produce better balanced meals and, consequently, an improved state of well-being. She lives in the Piedmont countryside, in Monferrato, and uses the flowers, aromatic herbs, and vegetables in her garden to make innovative sauces and condiments, as well as decorations for her dishes. She always allows herself to be guided by the evolution of the seasons and her knowledge of the fruits of the earth. In recent years, she has written several titles for White Star Publishers with enthusiasm and creativity.

WHITE STAR PUBLISHERS

WS White Star Publishers® is a registered trademark property of White Star s.r.l.

© 2021 White Star s.r.l.
Piazzale Luigi Cadorna, 6
20123 Milan, Italy
www.whitestar.it

ISBN 978-88-544-1744-1
1 2 3 4 5 6   25 24 23 22 21

Translation: TperTradurre s.r.l. - Editing: Abby Young

Printed in Serbia